Orig
Mirror Mayhem

Alex Woolf ■ Jonatronix

OXFORD
UNIVERSITY PRESS

Chapter 1 – The talent contest

Greenville's Got Talent!

Can you sing, dance or tell jokes?

Whatever your talent is, we'd love to see it.

Here's your chance to show off your skills and maybe even win a prize.

The Greenville School Talent Contest will be held on the last day of term.

Everyone is welcome to enter. See your teacher for details.

"We have to enter this!" Cat said. She was gathered with her friends, Max, Ant and Tiger, around the poster in the school corridor.

"I'm in," said Ant.

"I'll play the drums," said Tiger.

"I could do an amazing science experiment," said Ant.

"I could juggle," said Cat excitedly. She took three things out of her rucksack – a pencil case, a tennis ball and an orange from her lunch box. Then she began tossing them up in the air and catching them, one after the other.

"Hey, you're really good!" laughed Tiger.

Cat began showing off, throwing the objects even higher – until she fumbled, and everything fell down with a clatter.

"Maybe I need some practice," she admitted.

"What will *you* do, Max?" asked Tiger.

"Um ... I don't think I'll enter," said Max quietly.

"Why not?" asked Ant.

Max shrugged. "I don't really have those kinds of talents."

"Rubbish!" said Cat. "You're brilliant at lots of different things."

"I'm just not sure what I could do. I'll think about it," sighed Max.

The others were quiet for a moment, not knowing what to say. Then Tiger spoke. "Well, will you at least help us find some costumes and props for our performances?"

"Of course!" smiled Max.

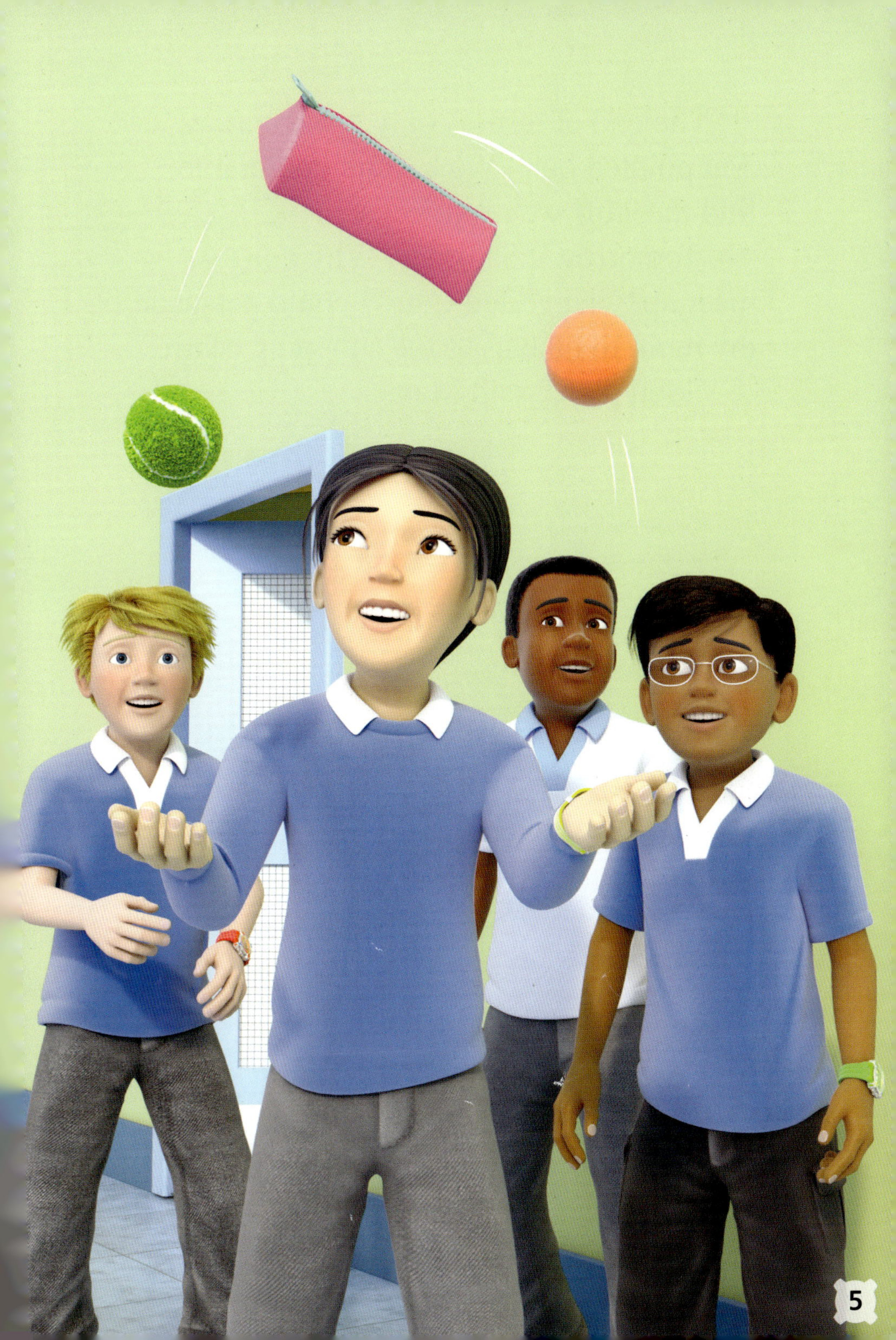

"The end of term is only a week away," Ant pointed out. "We haven't got long to find the stuff we need."

"Tomorrow's Saturday. Why don't we meet up?" suggested Cat. "I could persuade my mum to take us to the shopping centre."

"Good plan," said Max.

Meanwhile …

Little did the friends know that someone was sneakily listening in to their conversation. In the secret underground headquarters of NASTI, a man in a purple suit was looking at a screen. His name was Dr X. The children's special watches really belonged to him … and he would stop at nothing to get them back.

Dr X smiled to himself.

"Aha, the children are going shopping. This is my chance to take back what is mine, while they are distracted," he said to himself.

Chapter 2 – The fancy dress shop

The next day, Cat's mum took the four friends shopping.

"Why don't you go window-shopping while I look for a laptop in the computer shop over there?" Cat's mum suggested. "I'll meet you by the fountain in twenty minutes."

"Great!" said Cat, and the friends went off to explore.

"Hey, check out *this* place!" said Tiger, stopping outside a fancy dress shop.

"I've never seen this shop before," said Max. "It must be new."

"I could wear that at the talent contest," said Ant, pointing to a scientist costume in the window display.

"I really like that clown costume," said Cat.

The four friends trooped into the shop.

"We'd like to try on some of the costumes in your window, please," Cat said to the shop owner. "The scientist and the clown."

"Certainly," she replied. "They're great, aren't they? Let me get them for you."

Soon, Cat and Ant were having fun trying on the costumes.

Max and Tiger rummaged through the shop for accessories. They found a pair of rubber gloves for Ant and some juggling clubs for Cat.

The friends paid for their costumes, before taking it turns to practise their acts.

The friends were enjoying themselves so much that they didn't notice that the shop had suddenly become very quiet.

"Where's the owner gone?" asked Ant after a while.

"She must have just popped out for a moment," said Cat.

Just then, Tiger's watch started flashing a warning. "Oh, no! Look over there!" he groaned.

The others looked, and gasped. A small green robot – an X-bot – was scuttling towards them from the other side of the shop. The friends had met something similar before. They knew that the robot was probably after their watches.

"There are two more over there!" said Cat, pointing towards two X-bots crawling along the top of a clothes rail. "They're surrounding us!"

"Here's another one!" yelled Ant as an X-bot leaped onto his leg. He kicked furiously until it fell off.

"*Now* what should we do?" asked Cat. "We're trapped."

Chapter 3 – The sneeze

"Let's shrink," suggested Ant. "Then we can hide from the X-bots underneath the costumes on that clothing rail."

The friends turned the dials on their watches. They pushed the X and …

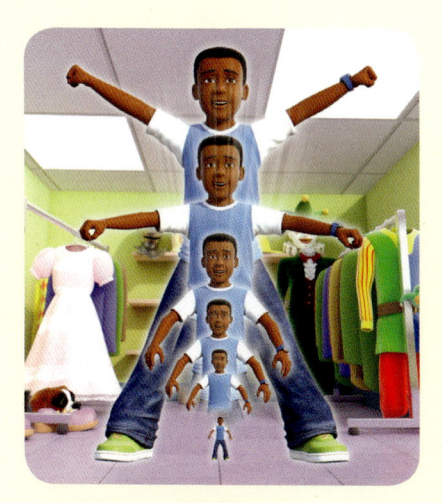

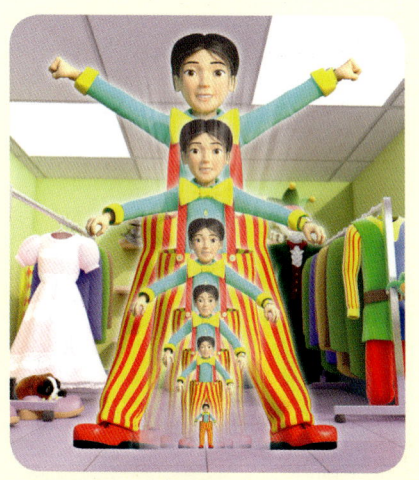

Suddenly, the shop seemed huge. Tall hats and giant boots towered over the friends. Huge animal masks stared down at them.

The X-bots looked much bigger now, but they seemed confused by the disappearance of the children.

Cat, Ant and Tiger scurried over to the clothing rack and took cover beneath the lacy hem of an enormous, old-fashioned dress. It was only then that they realized someone was missing.

"Where did Max go?" asked Ant.

"I've no idea," said Cat. "I'm sure he was here a minute ago."

The friends had no time to worry though, as one of the X-bots was approaching fast. They could hear its metallic footsteps getting louder. *CLUNK! CLUNK! CLUNK! CLUNK!*

The friends tried to stay as quiet as possible. Cat was finding it hard to breathe under all the dusty lace. Her eyes were beginning to water. With a sinking heart, she realized she was about to sneeze.

"Aaah … aaah …"

Cat couldn't stop herself. She clamped her hand over her mouth, but it was too late.

Ah-chooo!!!!

The red eyes of the X-bot lit up. It had heard her!

"Run!" cried Tiger.

The three friends sprinted out across the shop floor. They could hear the urgent, clanking sound of the X-bot as it came after them.

"To the counter!" shouted Cat.

Cat, Ant and Tiger began to clamber up the side of the counter, which towered above them like a cliff. They grabbed on to the drawer handles to pull themselves up.

"I hope the X-bots aren't good climbers," panted Ant.

To their surprise, they found Max waiting for them at the top. He was waving at them from the far end of the counter.

The friends started to run towards him – and immediately crashed straight into something solid!

"Wh-what just happened?" groaned Ant, rubbing his head.

"Where's Max?" asked Tiger, nursing his arm.

"Over here!" shouted Max.

Cat, Ant and Tiger turned around. Max was now at the *other* end of the counter. How had he got there so fast?

Chapter 4 – Mirror, mirror

Cat was the first person to work out what had happened. She tapped the shiny glass wall they had just crashed into. "It's a mirror!" she said.

The friends ran to join the real Max. The creaking sound of the X-bot climbing up the side of the counter was getting louder by the minute. Quickly, they hid behind the cash register and watched as a X-bot's head appeared over the counter top.

The cash register blocked the X-bot's view of the children, but when it looked in the mirror, it could see them hiding. It lurched towards the reflections and stretched out its metal pincer arms to grab them … *CRASH!* The X-bot collided with the mirror and fell on its back.

Ant cheered. The X-bot waggled its limbs in the air helplessly.

19

"That robot will get up again soon!" warned Tiger.

"I've got an idea," said Max. "Give me a hand." They all raced over to the mirror and began heaving it to the other end of the counter. Then they positioned it right at the very end of the countertop.

By now, the X-bot was back on its feet and looking around for them.

The friends quickly ducked down behind the cash register – except for Max. He remained standing in front of the mirror.

"What are you doing?" whispered Cat. "It'll see you."

Sure enough, the X-bot soon spotted Max, and began scuttling towards him at top speed.

"It's going to get you!" cried Tiger.

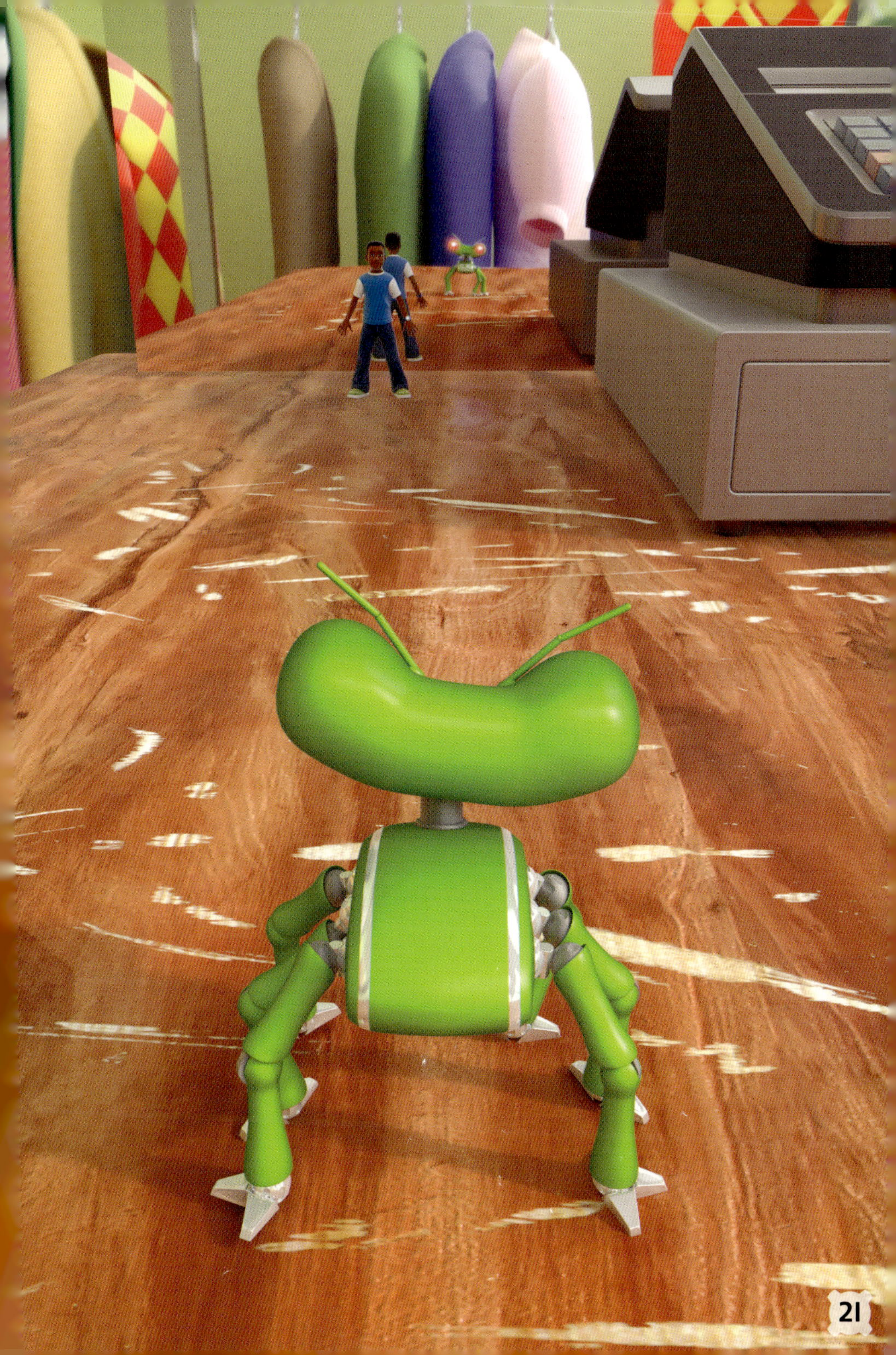

But Max stayed where he was – until the last moment. Then he moved to one side, quickly pushing the mirror away.

The X-bot couldn't stop and went toppling over the edge of the counter. The friends watched as it crashed onto the floor below.

"The reflection in the mirror made the counter look much longer than it was," said Ant. "The X-bot couldn't stop in time. Very clever, Max."

"We need to get out of here," said Tiger. "Let's head for the door."

The friends climbed down the side of the counter again. The shop door was far away and four more X-bots were blocking the way.

Chapter 5 – Tricks and illusions

"You saw how I tricked the X-bot up on the counter with the mirror," said Max. "We can do something similar with these X-bots." He pointed to a tall mirror leaning against the wall. "See how one of them is facing that mirror? Now watch this."

Max stood opposite the mirror. "Now you see me!" he called.

The X-bot lurched towards Max's reflection and smashed right into the mirror!

"Awesome!" cheered Cat.

The friends now knew what they had to do.

Cat ran over to another mirror and stood behind it. Peeping out, she called "Now you see me!" to one of the X-bots.

The X-bot stomped towards her, but before it could reach her, she ducked back behind the mirror.

"Now you don't!" called Cat.

The X-bot was left staring at itself in the mirror, wondering how Cat had turned into an X-bot! Cat quickly called out from the other side of the mirror and headed for the door.

Nearby there was another small mirror that people used when they tried on boots and shoes. Ant peeped out from behind it and called the last X-bot: "Now you see me!"

The X-bot charged at him and ran right into the mirror.

"Now you don't!" Ant shouted as he ran for the door.

25

Meanwhile, Tiger was trying to think of a way to get past the remaining X-bot which was lurking near the shop door.

Suddenly, he had an idea. Looking around, he found a bouncy ball that was the right size. By pushing the ball along the floor and walking at just the right speed, Tiger could hide from the X-bot *and* escape at the same time!

The ball rolled across the floor and up to the door in full view of the X-bot. The robot stopped and stared at it, but then trundled away to look somewhere else.

"Now you *don't* see me," Tiger whispered to himself.

Quickly, Tiger climbed through the letterbox to join his friends waiting outside. They had made it!

Chapter 6 – The magic show

Later that day, the friends met up at Tiger's house.

"You were brilliant today, Max!" said Cat.

Ant nodded in agreement. "Yeah, the way you outwitted those X-bots with mirrors and stuff. It was amazing."

Max grinned shyly. "Yeah, well, I've always loved optical illusions and magic tricks."

This gave Tiger an idea. "Hey, Max! Maybe you could perform a magic show at the talent contest. I've even got a top hat you could borrow. It's here somewhere ... "

Max looked at him. "You know, I never thought of that. Do you think I could?"

"Of course!" the others chorused. Tiger disappeared and then reappeared with the hat.

"Thanks, Tiger," said Max. "I'll get practising!"

A week later …

The school hall was packed for the talent contest. The whole school was there to watch or take part in the performances.

Cat juggled for three minutes without dropping her clubs, Tiger's drum performance was a great success and Ant's homemade volcano was superb.

The last performer on stage was Max. He made balls disappear and then reappear in unexpected places. He named playing cards he couldn't possibly have seen. He made a cup appear to float in mid-air and finally made a hoop rise up a string. He was amazing!

Max got the biggest applause of the night, and the loudest cheers came from his friends Cat, Ant and Tiger.

Mrs Mills didn't take long to decide who the winner was that evening.

"First prize in the Greenville School Talent Contest goes to … Max!"

Then she handed Max a golden trophy.

Meanwhile …

In the secret underground headquarters of NASTI, Dr X was trying not to lose his temper. "I can't believe it! You were fooled by a silly trick with mirrors!" he fumed at his X-bots. "What you see in a mirror isn't real. It's a reflection! Do you understand? Now reflect on *that!*"